It's Vital to Recycle!

Alex and Sarah were using the Internet
to find out more about recycling.
"Look at this," said Alex. "It says that
if people recycle it can save energy."
"I bet people don't know that,"
said Sarah.

"People should put papers, cans and plastic bottles in recycling boxes," said Alex. "They can be collected by the bin men."

"It's bin night tonight," said Sarah. "Let's check who is recycling."

OVER AND OUT

Contents

Haydn Middleton

Story illustrated by
Leo Hartas

Heinemann

In this story

 Alex

 Sarah

Tricky words

- Internet
- recycling
- energy
- plastic
- collected
- buried
- vital
- cardboard

Introduce these tricky words and help the reader when they come across them later!

Story starter

Alex and Sarah care about the environment. They are members of a green kids' club, and they are always looking for ways to encourage people to 'think green'! One day Alex and Sarah were in the library, using the Internet to find out more about recycling. They found a website that showed it is vital to recycle.

Alex and Sarah set off to check the bins. The first bin they saw had newspapers in it.

"Don't they know that newspapers can be recycled?" said Sarah as she put them in the recycling box.

"All the stuff in bins gets buried in landfill sites," said Sarah, "but the problem is we're filling up all our landfill sites."

"People need to know that it's vital to recycle!" said Alex.

"Look at that bin next door," said
Sarah. "There is a cardboard box
in it. Cardboard should go in the
recycling box."

Alex went over to the bin.

"But there's no recycling box to
put it in," he said.

Alex and Sarah knew what they had to do.

"We must tell these people to use their recycling box," said Alex.

"OK. Let's knock on the door," said Sarah.

But the woman who opened the door
was very cross.
"*I* didn't put any cardboard in my bin,"
she said. "Someone else must have put
it there. This isn't my problem."
Then she slammed her door.

"She's wrong," Sarah said to Alex.
"This is a problem for everyone.
If we don't recycle we will drown in
our own rubbish!"
"But maybe someone else *did* use
her bin," said Alex.
He was pointing down the street.
Other bins had cardboard boxes in
them too.

"You're right," said Sarah. "And they're all mobile phone boxes." "It's a bit funny that everyone in this street got a new mobile phone at the same time," said Alex. "What is going on?"

What do **you** think is going on?

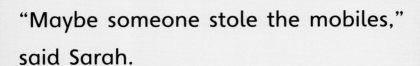

"Maybe someone stole the mobiles," said Sarah.

"And now they're dumping the boxes!" said Alex.

"There's a man just down the street," said Alex. "Let's ask him if he has seen anyone dumping cardboard boxes."
Sarah grabbed Alex's arm.
"No!" she whispered. "*He's* the one doing the dumping!"

Sarah was right. The man dumped his last box before running away.

Alex and Sarah got on their bikes and rode after him. He went into a house and slammed the door.

"The police might be very interested in this," said Alex.

Sarah called the police and asked if any mobiles had gone missing. "Yes!" said a police officer. "Someone stole a hundred from a van just last night. We're on our way."

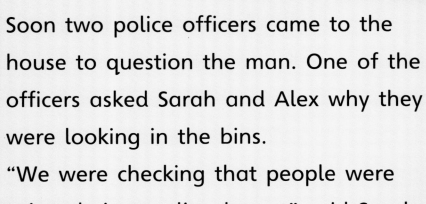

Soon two police officers came to the house to question the man. One of the officers asked Sarah and Alex why they were looking in the bins.

"We were checking that people were using their recycling boxes," said Sarah. "Lucky for us you're so green!" said the police officer.

Quiz

Text Detective

- Why did Sarah and Alex knock on the woman's door?
- Why do you think the man put only one mobile phone box in each bin?

Word Detective

- **Phonic Focus:** Identifying and spelling word endings
  Page 14: Find three past tense verbs ending with 'ed'.
  What sound does each 'ed' ending make?
  (dumped, t; slammed, d; interested, ed)
- Page 10: Why is the word 'did' in bold print?
- Page 11: Find a word that means 'odd'.

Super Speller

Read these words:

asked   stole   someone

Now try to spell them!

HA! HA! HA!

 Q How do you communicate with a fish?

A Drop him a line!

Find out about

- Different ways people send messages

Tricky words

- message
- pigeons
- soldiers
- Ancient Greeks
- nonsense
- thickness
- semaphore
- country

Introduce these tricky words and help the reader when they come across them later!

Text starter

How can you keep in touch with a friend? You can talk on your mobile phone, send a text or send an e-mail. But long ago people sent messages by banging drums, lighting fires or sending pigeons. People even used flags to send messages.

Keep in Touch

You are at home.

Your friend is at his home.

How can you get in touch?

You can talk on your mobile,

send a text or send an e-mail.

But how did people in the past

keep in touch?

Send a message

Long ago, people sent messages by banging on drums or lighting big fires. People far away heard the drums or saw the fire. They knew what these messages meant. Often the messages meant 'Help!'

Only very simple messages could be sent by drums or fire.

Later on, people sent written messages. Riders on horses would carry the messages for miles and miles.

Pigeons carried messages even faster. In the past, soldiers took pigeons with them to send messages back home. They tied the message to the pigeon's leg. Then the pigeon flew home.

Keep your message secret

Often you didn't want people to read your message.

The Ancient Greeks rolled a narrow strip of paper around and around a stick. They wrote their message down the stick, on the paper. Then they unrolled the paper.

Now the message looked like nonsense!

They sent the paper strip to their friend, who had a stick of the same thickness. The friend would roll the paper around the stick and read the message.

If you didn't have a stick of the right thickness, you couldn't read the message.

Flag a friend

Sometimes you could see a person, but they were too far away to hear you. People would use flags to send them a message.

This is called semaphore.

If you held the flags one way, it meant the letter A. If you held them another way, it meant the letter B — and so on.

You could send messages right across the country this way, but it would take a long time!

Tap to keep in touch

Before we had phones, people sent messages along wires by tapping.

A man called Samuel Morse made up a code.

A short tap made a dot and a long tap made a dash. Mixes of dots and dashes made up all the letters from A to Z.

Your friend heard your taps, turned the dots and dashes into words – and got your message!

Dot dot dot dash dash dash dot dot dot. This means 'SOS' or 'Help'!

Faster and faster

The first telephones were big, and you had to ask an operator to connect your call.

Now mobile phones are tiny and you can call someone directly. You can send them text messages and even send photographs over the phone!

Lots of people now use computers to keep in touch. You can send e-mails to friends all over the world.

You can also send 'instant messages'. As soon as you send one of these, it gets to your friend's computer.

That really *is* keeping in touch!

The Internet

The Internet is great for keeping in touch. You can make a 'blog' on the Internet, and all your friends can read it.

But remember not to put any secrets in it!

We keep inventing new ways to keep in touch.

First there were phones, and then there were computers. Now you can talk to your friends using your computer – and see them on your screen!

What will we invent next?

Quiz

Text Detective

- How did soldiers use pigeons to send messages?
- How do you keep in touch with your friends?

Word Detective

- **Phonic Focus:** Identifying and spelling word endings.
  Page 22: Find three past tense verbs ending with 'ed'.
  What sound does each 'ed' ending make?
  (rolled, d; unrolled, d; looked, t)
- Page 20: Find three plural nouns.
- Page 21: Find a word that means 'fixed'.

Super Speller

Read these words:

heard   computer   wrote

Now try to spell them!

HA! HA! HA!

Q What do you get if you cross a parrot with a homing pigeon?

A A bird that asks the way home!